W9-AST-016

DISCARD

Form 178 rev. 01-07

Chicago Public Library
Beverly Branch
1962 W. 95th Street
Chicago, IL 60643

# FIESTA!

# MONGOLIA

GROLIER

An Imprint of Scholastic Library Publishing
Danbury, Connecticut

Published for Grolier
an imprint of Scholastic Library Publishing
Old Sherman Turnpike, Danbury, Connecticut 06816
by Marshall Cavendish Editions
an imprint of Marshall Cavendish International
1 New Industrial Road, Singapore 536196

Copyright © 2004 Times Media Pte Ltd, Singapore
Second Grolier Printing 2006

All rights in this book are reserved. No part of this book may be used or reproduced in any manner
whatsoever or transmitted in any form or by any means, electronic or mechanical, including photocopying,
recording, or any information storage and retrieval system, without written permission from the copyright owner
except in the case of brief quotations embodied in critical articles and reviews. For information, address
the publisher: Scholastic Library Publishing, Old Sherman Turnpike, Danbury, Connecticut 06816.

Set ISBN: 0-7172-5788-6
Volume ISBN: 0-7172-5796-7

**Library of Congress Cataloging-in-Publication Data**
Mongolia.
p. cm.—(Fiesta!)
Summary: Discusses the festivals and holidays of Mongolia and how the songs, food,
and traditions associated with these celebrations reflect the culture of the people.
1. Festivals—Mongolia—Juvenile literature. 2. Mongolia—Social life and customs—Juvenile literature.
[1. Festivals—Mongolia. 2. Holidays—Mongolia. 3. Mongolia—Social life and customs.]
I. Grolier (Firm). II. Fiesta! (Danbury, Conn.)
GT4886.M65M65     2004
394.26517'3—dc21          2003044848

*For this volume*
Author: Grace Chia
Editor: Daphne Rodrigues
Designer: Lynn Chin
Production: Nor Sidah Haron
Craft and Recipes produced by Stephen Russell

Printed by Everbest Printing Co. Ltd

Adult supervision advised for all crafts and recipes,
particularly those involving sharp instruments and heat.

R03262 48182

BEV

# CONTENTS

# MONGOLIA:

*Slightly smaller in size than Mexico, Mongolia is a land of mountains and desert. The climate is dry, with little snow or rain. Winters are long and very cold, while summers are short and mild.*

Uvs

Altai Mountains

◄ **Yaks** are important animals in the daily lives of Mongolian herders. Yak milk is used to make "white foods" such as yogurt, butter, and cheese. The yak's hide is made into leather, and its flesh is eaten.

▶ **A *ger*** is a large tent in which a Mongolian family lives. The tent cover is made of white felt, and the frame is made of wood. The *ger* suits the lifestyle of nomadic Mongolians. It is easy to put up and to take down when the family needs to move to a new place.

Hövsgöl

ULAANBAATAR

RUSSIA

Karakorum

MONGOLIA

Mongolian Steppe

CHINA

Gobi Desert

▲**Erdene Zuu** is the oldest Buddhist monastery in Mongolia. It is located in the ancient capital, Karakorum. Erdene Zuu took more than three centuries to build, starting in 1586. The monastery preserves many cultural treasures, and its name means "Hundred Treasures."

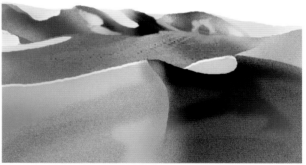

▲**The Gobi Desert** makes up about a third of Mongolia's land in the south. It has large sand dunes and plains. Many kinds of animals live there, such as gazelles, geckos, wild camels, and Gobi bears. Even dinosaurs may once have lived in the Gobi Desert. Scientists have found dinosaur bones there.

# RELIGIONS

**The main religion in Mongolia is a form of Buddhism called Lamaism. There are also Christians and Muslims in Mongolia. Other Mongolians practice shamanism.**

LAMAISM became the state religion of Mongolia in 1586. The king at that time built a monastery called Erdene Zuu in Karakorum. He made the monastery the center of Lamaism in Mongolia.

*This is a sculpture of Tara, the goddess of compassion and protection. Lamaists turn to her in times of trouble.*

Lamaism is closely related to Tibetan Buddhism. Followers of Lamaism, called Lamaists, believe that after we die, we are born into another life. They also believe that how we live now affects our next life, and that one day we will reach a state of perfection and will be released from the cycle of death and rebirth. Lamaists make up 96 percent of the people of Mongolia.

Lamaists worship by saying prayers, singing hymns, and performing rituals. On special days they offer food at the monasteries. The largest monastery in Mongolia is Gandan. It is located in the capital city, Ulaanbaatar.

*Lamaists may pray with beads. There are 108 beads on a string; shorter strings have fewer beads.*

CHRISTIANITY came to Mongolia with Persian missionaries in the eighth century. Since then more Christian missionaries have come from many other countries to spread the teaching of Jesus Christ throughout Mongolia.

Today thousands of Mongolians are Christian, and they can even read the Bible translated into Mongolian.

ISLAM is an important religion in the western Altai region of Mongolia. Most Muslims (followers of Islam) in Mongolia are ethnic Kazakhs.

Muslims in Mongolia follow some traditional Islamic practices. They also perform some rituals from their ancient religion — shamanism — and believe in superstitions such as the evil eye.

SHAMANISM is the oldest religion in Mongolia. It began in prehistoric times and was a big part of life for the Mongols (the ancient people of Mongolia) up to the 16th century.

Today some Mongolians still practice shamanism. They believe that spirits live in the earth and in animals. They respect nature and try to live in harmony with the environment. In return, they believe that the spirits of their ancestors and of animals will provide for their needs.

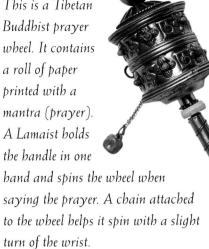

*This is a Tibetan Buddhist prayer wheel. It contains a roll of paper printed with a mantra (prayer). A Lamaist holds the handle in one hand and spins the wheel when saying the prayer. A chain attached to the wheel helps it spin with a slight turn of the wrist.*

# GREETINGS FROM **MONGOLIA!**

The people of Mongolia are called Mongolians. There are about 2.7 million Mongolians. Of them more than 80 percent are ethnic Mongols. Other ethnic groups in Mongolia include Kazakhs, Chinese, and Russians. The official language of Mongolia is Khalkha, a Mongolian dialect. The Mongolian language group belongs to the Ural-Altaic language family, which also includes Finnish, Hungarian, Kazakh, and Turkish. Not many Mongolians speak anything other than Mongolian or Russian. Kazakhs also speak the Kazakh language. Mongolian words can be spelled using the Roman alphabet. When reading Romanized Mongolian words, stress double vowels, such as "ii" or "aa," and roll the "r"s.

## How do you say ...

Hello
**Sain bainuu**

Goodbye
**Bayartai**

Thank you
**Bayarlaa**

My name is ...
**Minii ner ...**

I'm sorry/Excuse me
**Uuchlaarai**

# NAADAM FESTIVAL

**Naadam is the most important festival of the year in Mongolia. Archers, horse racers, and wrestlers test their skills in friendly competition. People wear colorful clothes to watch the games.**

*A Naadam racehorse wears this bright-colored ornament on its forehead, right between the eyes.*

Every summer in Mongolia people celebrate a big festival called Eriin Gurvan Naadam — this means "Three Manly Sports," but women and children also take part in the festival.

The Naadam festival is celebrated in different parts of Mongolia, but the biggest celebration is in the capital, Ulaanbaatar. Naadam takes place from July 11 to July 13. It marks the anniversary of the 1921 revolution, when the first Mongolian government was formed.

During Naadam the best Mongolian athletes compete in three popular sports: archery, wrestling, and horse racing. These sports celebrate the skills of the ancient Mongols, who were great riders and archers on the battlefield.

ARCHERY began in Mongolia thousands of years ago. The ancient Mongol warriors each carried a curved bow and quivers full of arrows.

Naadam archers shoot at small leather cylinders arranged in a row on the

*In the archery event the targets are lined up some 200 to 250 feet away from the archers.*

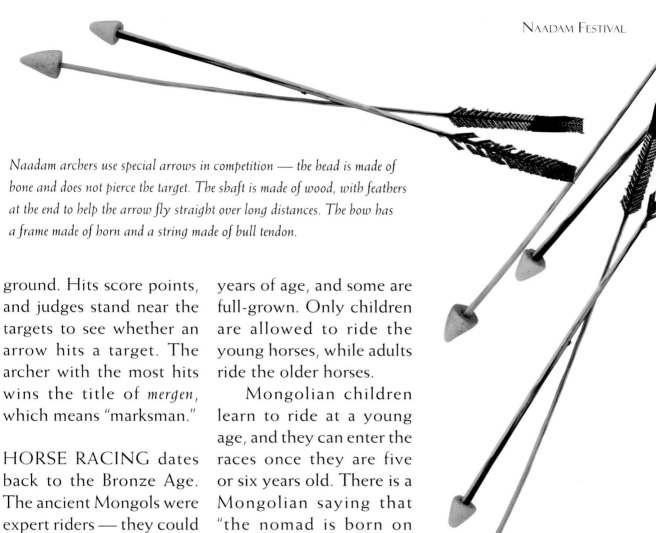

*Naadam archers use special arrows in competition — the head is made of bone and does not pierce the target. The shaft is made of wood, with feathers at the end to help the arrow fly straight over long distances. The bow has a frame made of horn and a string made of bull tendon.*

ground. Hits score points, and judges stand near the targets to see whether an arrow hits a target. The archer with the most hits wins the title of *mergen*, which means "marksman."

HORSE RACING dates back to the Bronze Age. The ancient Mongols were expert riders — they could ride and shoot arrows at the same time.

The Naadam race is between 9 and 18 miles long. Both the horse and the rider need a lot of skill to cross rivers and hills, valleys and plains.

The horses are chosen for training and fed a special diet at least one month before the festival. Some are as young as two years of age, and some are full-grown. Only children are allowed to ride the young horses, while adults ride the older horses.

Mongolian children learn to ride at a young age, and they can enter the races once they are five or six years old. There is a Mongolian saying that "the nomad is born on horseback." The riders are able to control how fast their horses run so that the horses have enough energy to finish the race.

Naadam riders wear light, comfortable clothes and decorate their horses with colorful ornaments.

Before the race begins, there is a parade of the riders on their horses. The horses circle the finish area three times, and the riders sing a mantra, or prayer. Then the horses get ready at the starting line; and when the signal is given, the riders drive their horses forward, raising a cloud of sand and dust.

A Naadam horse rider wears a number tag. The number appears on both the front and back panels, so that the judges can keep track of the rider during the competition.

At the end of the race the first five horses, called "Airag Five," are sprinkled with *airag*, or fermented horse milk. The winning horse gets the title "Ahead of 10,000 Horses."

Even the last horse gets a title — "Rich Stomach." The spectators cheer on the last rider to encourage him to take part again the next year.

WRESTLING is the main Naadam event, with 512 participants, all men. There are nine rounds of matches in the whole tournament. During the match two men wrestle each other until one falls or a part of his body other than his hands or feet touches the ground. To win the tournament, a wrestler has to beat his opponents in all nine rounds. If he loses one round, he is out of the tournament.

The title that a wrestler receives depends on how many rounds he wins. If he wins five rounds, he is called "Falcon." Seven rounds, and he is called "Elephant." The overall winner is called "Lion." A

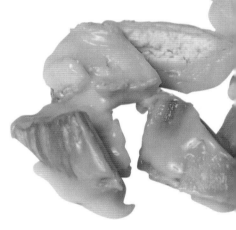

Cheese, like other homemade dairy food products, is very popular during the Naadam festival. Mongolians make different kinds of cheese using milk from their animals.

wrestler who wins the national tournament two years in a row earns the title "Giant."

Mongolian wrestlers wear tight-fitting silk shorts, long silk sleeves joined at the back across the shoulders, and high leather boots called *gutal* (the left and right boot are the same shape). They also wear a velvet cap with four sides and a pointed top.

Before the tournament the contestants perform a special dance, with their arms stretched out like the wings of a falcon. At the end of a match the loser walks under the arms of the winner and unties his vest. Then the winner does the falcon dance around the state flag. The winner gets biscuits as his prize. He tastes a biscuit and gives the rest to the spectators.

But the winner's real prize is national fame. At the next Naadam he will be known and called not only by his own name but also by his title of honor.

*These postage stamps show Mongolian wrestlers in the traditional cap, sleeves, shorts, and boots.*

*Before the Naadam festival Mongolians prepare a lot of* airag, *the national drink. It is made from horse milk left in a large bowl or pot overnight. The sugar in the milk turns into alcohol.*

# ERKHII MERGEN

*There is a part of the marmot's body that Mongolians do not eat.*
*They call it "man's meat." This refers to the flesh of the world's greatest archer,*
*who saved the world from the fire of seven suns before turning into a marmot.*

LONG AGO there were seven suns in the sky. The heat was so strong that the rivers dried up, the animals hid in their burrows, and the plants died. The people looked for a young man named Erkhii Mergen. He was the greatest archer in the world, and he never missed a target.

"Erkhii Mergen, help us!" the people cried, "Shoot down the seven suns, or everything will die!"

Young Erkhii promised, "I will shoot down the seven suns using only seven arrows. If I do not succeed, I will cut off my thumbs and live in a hole."

The next morning Erkhii set out to find a place on a hill and waited for the suns to pass above. The fearless archer drew his bow and shot an arrow. One by one his arrows shot down the suns, until only one was left. Erkhii prepared to hit his final target. He aimed, held his breath, and released the seventh arrow.

Suddenly, a swallow got in the way, and the arrow forked its tail. (That is why swallows have a forked tail.) The arrow fell to earth — it had missed the last sun.

Erkhii swore to kill the swallow. He commanded his horse to chase the bird, but the horse replied, "Master, I will chase that swallow until the sun sets. If I cannot catch up with it, you may cut off my legs."

They chased the swallow across the Mongolian steppe, but the horse could not keep up. Then the sun began to set, and the sky grew red. Erkhii cut off the horse's front legs and threw them in the desert. Instantly, the horse turned into a jerboa, a jumping mouse. (That is why the jerboa's front legs are shorter than its hind legs.)

Keeping his promise to the people, Erkhii cut off his thumbs. He turned into a marmot (that is why a marmot has only four claws), found a deep dark hole, and lived on old grass.

# MONGOLIAN NEW YEAR

*The Mongolian New Year is called Tsagaan Sar (White Month). It takes place in January or February, marking the end of winter and the beginning of spring. The exact date of the festival changes every year, following the lunar calendar.*

This is a Mongolian *del, complete with cap, sash, and boots.*

Tsagaan Sar, like Naadam, is a big national holiday in Mongolia. People start preparing for Tsagaan Sar at least one month before the festival begins.

It is a custom to wear a new *del* (the traditional Mongolian attire) on New Year's Day. Parents buy or make new clothes for themselves, their children, and other family members. They also stock up on food and buy presents.

On the eve of the new year relatives gather for the last dinner of the year. It is called *bituun*, which means "to close down." Before Mongolians greet the new year, they have to wrap up all their business from the past year, pay off their debts, and rebuild poor relationships.

The women of the household usually do the cooking for the *bituun* table. Most of the food is dried, steamed, or boiled: boiled lamb, hundreds of steamed dumplings called *buuz*, and dairy foods such as cheese.

Alcoholic drinks and tea are also prepared.

When the table is set, the guests straighten their clothes, put on their caps,

*Mongolians make raisin rice for the New Year's eve dinner. They cook rice with sugar, butter, and raisins.*

*The first thing Mongolians do to prepare for Tsagaan Sar is to clean the ger and the cattle sheds.*

and sit around the table. The host takes a sip of tea before the hostess begins serving it to the guests. She serves the elders first and the children last.

Next, the host slices the lamb and gives each person a piece. Only then are the other dishes served, and the family enjoys the feast late into the night.

Milk tea accompanies the meal. The older relatives have alcoholic drinks, such as *airag* and milk vodka.

# BUUZ

*Buuz* is a Mongolian dish. Mongolians love lamb and usually make *buuz* with it, but you can also use beef.

### SERVES 4 TO 6
$1^1/_2$ pounds minced lamb
$^1/_2$ tsp black pepper
$1^1/_2$ tsps salt
$^1/_2$ tsp paprika, marjoram, or cumin
$1^1/_2$ pounds plain flour
$^1/_2$ cup water

**1** Marinate the lamb with the pepper, some salt, and a sprinkle of spice. Leave in the fridge for one hour.

**2** To make the dough, mix the flour with the remaining salt. Adding a little water at a time, knead the mixture into a firm dough. Cover with a damp cloth, and set aside.

**3** Use a rolling pin to flatten the dough to a thickness of $^1/_{10}$ inch. Use a small bowl to cut out circles of dough 4 to 6 inches in diameter.

**4** Place a teaspoonful of the meat in the center of each dough circle. Wrap the dough around the meat, and press the edges of the dough at the top to form a bundle, leaving a gap for steam to escape when cooking.

**5** Put the dumplings in a steamer half-filled with water. Boil the water, and steam the dumplings for about 10 to 15 minutes, until the meat is cooked. Serve warm on a plate.

*The caps of these little teapots have the figures of four of the 12 animals in the lunar horoscope: rabbit, rooster, horse, and snake.*

The next morning the whole family is awake by 6 A.M. Everyone gets into their new clothes and gathers outside the *ger*. They raise their hands to greet the first sunrise of the new year. Nature is a big part of Mongolian life, and many Mongolian folk songs are about the natural environment. One such song is called *Dorven Dalai*, or "Four Seas."

Afterward, the younger members of the family will greet their elders. The oldest member of the family is greeted first. In a Mongolian greeting two people hold each other's arms, wish each other health and happiness, and kiss on the cheek.

An important present during Tsagaan Sar is a long piece of blue, white, or yellow silk. It is called a *khadag*, and the younger relatives give it to their elders with a cup of wine in the right hand.

After the greetings everyone goes back into the *ger* for another feast. Gifts are exchanged, and then the meal begins. Again there is *buuz*, raisin rice, boiled meat, and other dishes. The host slices the meat and serves the oldest person first. Everyone drinks at least three small cups of tea, *airag*, or a milk drink during the meal.

During the rest of the day the family visits other relatives, neighbors, and friends. At every home people exchange gifts and eat *buuz*. Visitors are fed well; the host believes this will bring the family prosperity through the year. The celebration goes on into the evening with songs and games.

Mongolians continue to exchange presents and wish one another well for at least the next two weeks.

*Mongolians treasure family ties and display photos of their family members at home.*

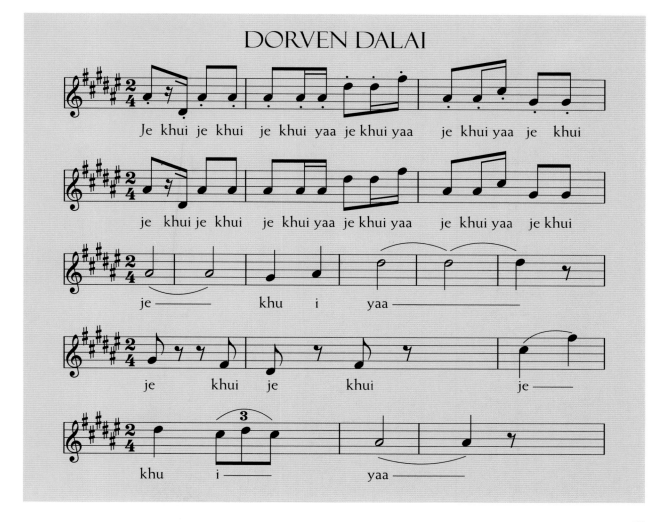

# MAKE A MONGOLIAN NOTEPAD COVER

## YOU WILL NEED
*Tracing paper*
*Pencil*
*Black, red, and yellow marker pens*
*Scissors*
*Glue*
*Plain red card 5 by 8 inches*
*Sheets of writing paper 5 by 7 inches*
*Hole puncher*
*Twine*

Mongolians decorate their new clothes, hats, and boots with a special embroidery design. Use this design to make an attractive cover for your notepad. Once you know how to make the design, you can decorate almost anything with it!

**1** Put the tracing paper over the design at the top of the facing page. Copy the outlines in pencil.

**2** Use the marker pens to fill in the pencil-drawn outlines. Follow the colors in the design on the facing page.

**3** Cut along the edge of the black box. Apply the glue on the reverse side, and paste the design on the red card.

**4** Fold a 1-inch flap on the top edge of the red card. Arrange the sheets of writing paper under the red card so that the edges fit in the flap.

**5** Make two holes in the flap side of the card and papers. Loop the holes using the twine, and tie a knot to bind the papers and the cover together.

# MAIDARI FESTIVAL

*This religious festival is celebrated during the lunar new year. The main attraction of the Maidari festival is a procession of thousands of people. They follow a cart carrying a statue of Maidari, the future Buddha.*

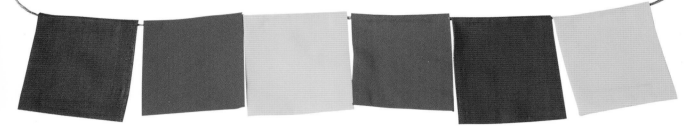

*Mongolians hang prayer flags across trees in the mountains and buildings in the cities.*

*The lotus appears very often in Buddhism, especially in relation to the gods and goddesses. It is a symbol of purity.*

Lamaists gather in the thousands at monasteries during the Maidari festival. They pray for hours and follow a statue of Maidari, the future Buddha, in a large, colorful procession.

The Maidari festival celebrates hope. It is believed that Maidari (Friendship), the future Buddha, will come at the end of time to return the world to its former glory. Mongolians celebrate this festival in the hope of receiving blessings and being reborn in the new world of the future.

Before the procession begins, some worshipers

*Scrolls are an ancient way of recording Buddhist scripture. During the Maidari festival the procession stops several times for scripture readings.*

20

carefully carry the statue of Maidari out of the temple. The statue may show Maidari standing or sitting on a lotus flower, or it may show Maidari holding a lotus flower.

The worshipers place the statue on a cart that is decorated with banners, ribbons, and prayer flags. There are mantras written on the prayer flags, and Mongolians hang the flags in the open, hoping that the winds will carry the benefits of the mantras to all the people and animals in the area.

There is a figure of a horse's head attached to the front of the cart. That makes it look as if a horse is pulling the cart. (But it is really monks who are pulling.) The rest of the crowd follows as close as they can — some people try to throw money at the foot of the statue.

*People used horses to pull carts in ancient times. Today Mongolians use a figure of a horse's head to represent the Maidari cart puller.*

## A SPECIAL PROCESSION

A special horse's head sits in the Museum of Fine Arts in Ulaanbaatar. It is no longer used during the Maidari festival, as it was in the early 20th century. The horse's head is carved from wood and covered with green velvet. It has a velvet bridle and copper fittings, and stands almost 35 inches high. Its mane is made from real horse hair that has been colored red.

In the early 20th century this special horse's head was attached to a cart used in the Maidari festival at the monastery of the Bogdo Gegen, the Lamaist leader, in Urga (the old name for Ulaanbaatar). The cart no longer exists. The Maidari festival at the Bogdo Gegen's monastery was one of Mongolia's biggest at that time. It was held on the last day of Tsagaan Sar.

Every year the procession would go around the Bogdo Gegen's monastery, stopping at specific places for the monks to chant prayers. The cart carried an image of the future Buddha sculpted by Zanabazar, the first Bogdo Gegen. The monks painted the cart in many colors and took good care of it and its fixtures and cargo.

21

# CREATION OF THE MIDDLE WORLD

*While Mongolians look to a new world ruled by Maidari, they tell this story about how the present world was created. Two brothers ruled the upper and lower worlds before the middle world — earth — was created.*

IN THE BEGINNING Father Heaven had two sons, Ulgen Tenger and Erleg Khan (or Erlik Khan). Ulgen became the lord of the upper world; Erleg became the lord of the lower world.

There was no land, only water. Ulgen asked a loon (a diving bird) to bring up mud from the water. The loon could not do it and was punished — its legs were broken. (To this day the loon cannot walk well.) Ulgen then asked a duck to bring up mud from the water. The duck made a small piece of land, and Ulgen fell asleep on it. Erleg saw his brother sleeping and tried to pull the ground from under him. But the more he pulled, the bigger the piece of land became. That is how the earth's land was created.

Ulgen then decided to create animals and people out of the mud. He made a dog to watch over the people. Erleg came to see the people, but the dog would not let him come near them.

The dog had no fur to keep it warm in the snow. Erleg said that if he could look at the people, he would give the dog a beautiful coat of fur. The dog agreed, and it got a shiny coat. But Erleg spat on the people and gave them diseases — they were no longer immortal.

Ulgen was shocked and angry to find his people damaged and his dog covered in fur. To punish the dog, Ulgen made its coat smelly and took away its voice. And from then on, the dog had to follow the people in order to get food.

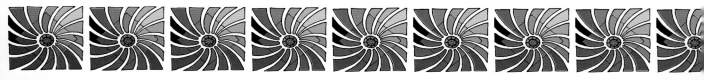

# HAIR-CUTTING CEREMONY

*Mongolian children traditionally have their first haircut at age three or five. This is celebrated in a ceremony that lasts all day, with a lot of eating, drinking, and singing.*

The hair-cutting ceremony is an old Mongolian tradition, especially among nomads. Parents do not cut a child's hair until the child is three or five years old, so little boys and girls all tie their hair in a pigtail.

This ceremony is a big event in a person's life — it is like a "graduation" from childhood. When a child is ready to have its first haircut, that means that he or she has come of age.

The ceremony usually takes place in the fall. That is when nomadic families are camped close together. Whenever there is a hair-cutting ceremony, the whole family celebrates, and relatives, neighbors, and friends are all invited to the *ger* on the big day.

Everyone takes part in the ceremony by snipping a small lock of the child's hair. Each guest gives the child a present, such as money, toys, biscuits, sugar

*At a hair-cutting ceremony the child carries a pair of scissors and a small silk bag. Each guest snips off a little of the child's hair and puts it in the bag.*

cubes, or tea bricks. (A tea brick is green or black tea leaves pressed into a block. That preserves the quality of the tea over a longer period. In ancient times tea was carried on camelback in the form of "bricks.")

Food is laid on tables in the *ger*, and the guests talk, laugh, and sing folk

*Guests at a hair-cutting ceremony may give money as a present.*

# SALTY TEA

### SERVES 8 to 10

*4 cups water*
*1 tbsp green tea*
*Salt to taste*
*4 cups milk*
*1 tbsp soft butter (optional)*

Mongolians drink tea all through the day. They drink black tea, green tea, rice tea, milk tea, and salty tea. Salty tea is a strong green tea mixed with salt and butter. It has a unique taste and smell that Mongolians love, especially during the long, cold winter.

**1** Boil the water, tea, and salt in a pot for four minutes.

**2** Add the milk, and boil again for about 30 seconds.

**3** Stir using a ladle. Scoop the tea, and slowly pour it back into the pot from a height of about 12 inches. That will make the tea bubbly.

**4** Add the butter, and let it melt into the tea. Serve in small cups.

*Sugar cubes are a practical gift. Mongolians use sugar to cook, or they may add it to tea.*

songs while enjoying the food. Tea is served, as well as alcoholic drinks made from horse, goat, or cow's milk. The host offers each guest a glass of vodka.

The guest takes the glass in the right hand (Mongolians consider it rude to use the left hand when serving or taking food or drink), takes a sip, and passes the glass back to the host. The host then serves another glass of the vodka to the next guest.

If an older relative cannot attend the hair-cutting ceremony, some hair is left on the child's head for the person to cut at a later date.

# TSAM CEREMONY

*Tsam masked dances are religious ceremonies performed by monks at large monasteries to chase away evil spirits. The main attraction of Tsam dances is the colorful masks of gods, demons, and animals.*

Tsam, meaning "masked dance," is an art form that spread to Mongolia from Tibet in the 18th century. The masks and costumes used by Tsam performers are based on characters from Buddhist legend. Tsam in Mongolia also borrows from the shaman traditions of the nomads.

In the 19th century many large monasteries were built in Mongolia. Each monastery held a Tsam performance every year. But in the 1930s communist rule put a stop to the celebration of Tsam in Mongolia.

Only in the 1990s did Mongolians start to revive the Tsam tradition. Older monks remembered the dances from before the days of communist rule. They began to teach the dances to younger monks.

A Tsam ceremony is made up of several dances that tell stories about the

*These stamps show a warrior defeating a demon. Stories about the triumph of good over evil are acted out by Tsam performers.*

lives of the gods and folk heroes. Tsam performers wear costumes and masks that represent these gods and people.

Characters include the mountain god, Garuda; Erleg Khan, the god of the realm of death, who has a frightful face and wears a crown of skulls; and the white-bearded lord of life, or White Old Man.

It takes a lot of skill to make a Tsam mask. The masks have to be big so that people watching the performance from far away can see the expressions on the masks.

The masks are made from papier-mâché; gold and precious stones are used as decoration. The strong basic colors include red, black, yellow, white, and blue. Mask artists in different regions of the country follow a different style according to the people's preference.

Music is an important part of a Tsam ceremony. Tsam dancers use gestures to tell the story, and they dance to music played by experienced musicians on gongs, trumpets, drums, and other instruments.

Mongolians' favorite musical instrument is the *morin huur*. It is a wooden fiddle with a long stem that ends with a carving of a horse's head.

Tsam dancers at each monastery are guided by a monk of high rank. They put a lot of effort into the practice sessions before each ceremony, because

they want to make sure that they do a good job playing their roles in the stories of the gods.

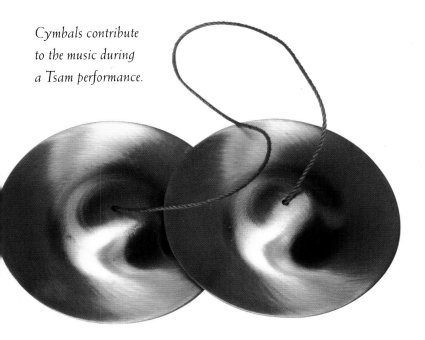

*Cymbals contribute to the music during a Tsam performance.*

*The* morin huur *is played at festivals and also for leisure.*

27

# FESTIVE WEAR

*Many Mongolians, especially in the countryside, wear their national costume everyday. But on special occasions Mongolians all over the country wear their traditional clothes.*

*These dolls are wearing traditional Mongolian wedding dress.*

Both men and women wear the traditional Mongolian outfit, or *del*. It is a gown made from wool or silk. It has long sleeves, no pockets, and often a sash that is tied around the waist. The wearer can tie a sheathed knife or a tobacco pouch to the sash, especially when riding a horse.

Some *del* are worn to work, while others are for festivals. Everyday *del* are cut from a simple pattern and are usually in a dull brown or gray. Festive or holiday *del* are made from bright-colored silk and are more elaborate.

There are also different kinds of *del* for different kinds of weather. There is a plain *del* that women in the countryside wear all year round. When it gets too cold, they wear warm clothes over the *del*. There is also a winter *del*. It is padded with sheep's wool on the inside.

*Del* makers use hand measurements, such as the length of a finger or the distance between the thumb and a finger on one hand. Each ethnic group has its own style of *del*, with a unique cut and special ornaments.

Mongolians also wear hats and boots to go with their *del*. Again, there are many kinds of hats and boots for different seasons of the year. The winter hat is made from fox fur, while the summer hat is made from velvet. The pointed front tip of the boots keeps warm air around the rider's toes, protecting them from the winter cold.

Many young people living in Mongolia's cities prefer to wear Western-style clothes such as jeans, shirts, and suits. But they do still wear *del* on special occasions such as concerts, weddings, and festivals.

# MAKE A MONGOLIAN HAT

## YOU WILL NEED

*Pencil*
*Scissors*
*Glue*
*Yellow card 11 by 17 inches*
*4 sheets white card 11 by 8 ¹/₂ inches*
*Adhesive tape*
*Orange and yellow crepe paper*
*5 feet feather fluff*

Traditional Mongolian hats are made of wool and have a broad rim, trimmed with fur. Here is a simple hat that you can make at home using easy-to-find materials.

**1** Draw a circle almost to the edges of the yellow card. Draw a smaller circle 6 inches inside the first circle. Cut along the lines. Remove a 5-inch section. The ring should look like a partly eaten doughnut.

**2** Draw a triangle with curved sides on each of the white cards. The triangles should be the same size. Cut out the triangles.

**3** Fold over two edges of each triangle. Glue the triangles together along the folded edges to form the crown of the hat.

**4** Using adhesive tape, join the two ends of the doughnut shape to form a rim. Stick the yellow rim around the bottom of the white crown using more adhesive tape.

**5** Cut four long strips of the orange and yellow crepe paper. Cut a V-shape into the lower end of each strip. Glue the other end of each strip to the back of the hat to form tails.

**6** Paste more crepe paper around the outside of the rim. Stick the feather fluff to the rim and the top of the crown.

29

# OVOO CEREMONY

*The **ovoo** ceremony is a sacred event during which people worship the spirits of nature. Mongolians hold **ovoo** ceremonies at different times of the year.*

The *ovoo* ceremony has its origins in ancient shaman traditions. Long before Buddhism came, nomads in Mongolia already had their own religion, called shamanism. Followers of shamanism believe that spirits live in the trees and animals, mountains and rivers. They respect and try to live in harmony with these spirits.

Today even Lamaists in Mongolia use shaman rituals. For example, many Mongolians worship the spirits of nature at an altar called an *ovoo*. They build this altar using branches, stones, bones, and other natural materials. People usually build an *ovoo* near a monastery on a mountain.

When people meet for an *ovoo* ceremony, they walk around the altar three times. They place offerings of milk, vodka, sweets, money, or pieces of cloth at the altar. Monks pray to the spirits, asking them to bless the people with good weather and a healthy herd.

*Mongolians build a shaman altar (below) by piling sticks and stones into a mound and tying pieces of cloth to the sticks. Flowers (above) and anything natural may be added to the altar.*

# WORDS TO KNOW

**Airag:** Fermented horse milk.

**Bituun:** Dinner on the eve of the Mongolian New Year.

**Buuz:** Mongolian dumplings filled with mutton or lamb. They are steamed or fried.

**Del:** The national costume of Mongolia. The *del* is a robe with long sleeves and is tied at the waist with a sash. Many Mongolians wear a *del* every day, while others wear it only on special holidays.

**Ger:** A large white felt tent used by Mongolian nomads. In the Russian language a *ger* is called a *yurt*.

**Khalkha:** The official language of Mongolia.

**Marmot:** A furry rodent similar to a groundhog.

**Monastery:** A place where monks live.

**Mongols:** The ancient people of Mongolia. Ethnic Mongols today make up more than 80 percent of the population of Mongolia.

**Nomadic:** Wandering, not settled. Nomads move their homes in search of pasture for their herds.

**Ovoo:** An altar of sticks and stones built to worship the spirits of the natural world.

**Quiver:** A case for carrying arrows. An archer slings a quiver on his back so that he can quickly reach for an arrow to string on his bow.

**Scripture:** Sacred writing.

**Shamanism:** An ancient religion in which people worship the spirits of nature.

**Steppe:** A vast area of flat land with no trees. Steppes are found in Asia and southeastern Europe.

**Tsagaan Sar:** Literally "White Month," the Mongolian New Year.

**White foods:** Traditional foods made by nomads using the milk of animals that they herd. Yogurt and white butter are examples of white foods.

---

## ACKNOWLEDGMENTS

WITH THANKS TO:
Joseph Frois, Yumi Ng, Poh Siew Hong, Lynelle Seow, Tracy Tan, and Yu Hui Ying for the loan of artifacts

PHOTOGRAPHS BY:
Haga Library, Japan (cover), Sam Yeo (p. 6 bottom, p. 7 top, p. 8 top, p. 10 bottom, p. 14 top, p. 16, p. 17, p. 20 top, p. 24 bottom, p. 27 right, p. 28), Yu Hui Ying (all others)

ILLUSTRATIONS BY:
Cake (p. 1, pp. 4-5, p. 7), Ong Lay Keng (p. 13), Lee Kowling (p. 23)

# SET CONTENTS